2 6 JAN 0 4 2

- 7 NOV 0 4 2

- 7 DEC 0 4 2

27 MAY 0 4 2

I.L.L. JAN '89.

KT-442-885

CLASS   8 2 1   WITHDRAWN

AUTHOR   MIL

TITLE

COPY   4

STIRLING DISTRICT LIBRARY

B
A

821
MIL

MONTY TULIPTHREAD
—A Spotted Dick Goblin—

With my little spotted handkerchief
And my little walking stick,
I'm off to gather Perdufkins
By the River Candlewycke.
At this time of the morning
With Moss-Goss in the sky
They say that some Perdufkins
Are nearly two feet high.
I'll take me six Perdufkins
Back to Molly My
And she will make a moggle dish
Of Fresh Perdufkin Pie.
And I will give my pussy-dog
A plate upon the roof
And when he's eaten his 'dufkin up
You'll hear him go meiow-woof!

FOSAKINS STICKLOOT
—A Goblin Singer—

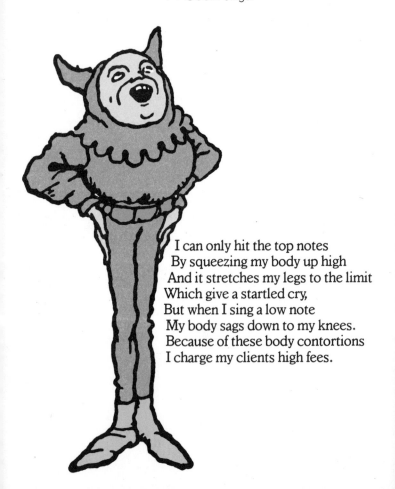

I can only hit the top notes
 By squeezing my body up high
 And it stretches my legs to the limit
Which give a startled cry,
But when I sing a low note
 My body sags down to my knees.
Because of these body contortions
I charge my clients high fees.

CRUET MACNIGHTSHADE
—A Street Singing Goblin—

La de da dee,
La de da de da,
I always look up when singing
Out in the street you see.

La de da de da
La de da dee dee,
Because of late they have been throwing
Buckets of water over me.

PRODDLE GILLYPONK
—A Goblin Chef—

What's happening to my dinner?
It's curling out of the pot;
I don't mind a dinner that's frisky
I'd rather it did that than not.

But this one is really alarming
For it jumped out on to the cat,
It dragged it out on to the landing
And gave it three falls on the mat

It's too soon to eat this dinner
I don't think it's properly dead,
I'll keep alive till it's ninety-two
Then shoot it in the head

MRS. MISTERMISS
—A Goblin Lady Cook—

I am a Lady Goblin Cook,
And that is why I'm in this book.
I've made a little pixie cake
I'm going to throw it in the lake,
For in that lake there is a fish
And pixie cake's his favourite dish.
I also gave one to my daughter,
Right now she's eating under water.

NORRIS PIGDRENCH
——— A Nothing Goblin ———

Please tell me the way to Nowhere,
That's where I want to go!
For somewhere out in Nowhere
There's a Ying Tong Iddle I Po.

I have come from Somewhere
Which is something miles away;
Perhaps when I get to Nowhere
The Fonnies will be at play.
Now, if I'm going Nowhere
I must carry a posey of dill
And the way to get to Nowhere
Is to hurry and stand quite still.

I'm on my way to Nowhere
Where the Golapins fill the air
And at the speed I'm standing still
By golly I'll soon be there.

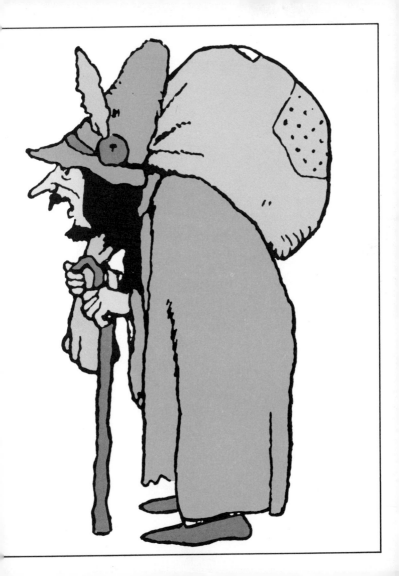

ZOOLEYTIFF STADDLE
—A Goblin Hurdy-Gurdy Player—

I'm a hurdy-gurdy man,
Come dance upon the Green,
Hear the tunes the Goblins write
For Fairy King and Queen.

The Music sounds like blackbirds,
Like willows in the wind
The little hoots of the bandicoots
And snad storms in the Sind.

I am the hurdy-gurdy man,
Dance to me while you may–
The sun is setting to the west
The darkness on its way.

NORRIS TREACLETRADE
A Goblin Jester

'Little Goblin Jester
What's in your spotted rag?
Is it a Pinkleponk Pudding
Or a hank of hair and a rag?'

'I'm afraid I cannot tell you!
The secret must be mine
But what*ever* it is,
It's not your biz
Until the clock strikes nine!'

Then on the stroke of nine o'clock
He placed it on the floor –
A blinding flash and explosion!
We never saw him anymore.

GRIZZLEGEE NUTPULP
A Demon Goblin Banjoist

I'm plucking on the middle
Of a one-string fiddle,
A-Plink-a-Plank
A-Plink-a-Plank-a-Plonk.

I'm trying to write a tune
It must come very soon,
A-Plink-a-Plank
A-Plink-a-Plank-a-Plonk.

I'll have another go
On my one-stringed fiddle-o,
A-Plink-a-Plank
A-Plink-a-Plank-a-Plonk.

Oh dearie dearie me,
A composer I won't be, so it's
Plink-a-Plank
A-Plink-a-Plank-a-Plonk.

SNEDRICK CRUMBB
—A Goblin Drummer—

My name is Snedrick Crumbb
I play a golden drum
Boom boom boom boom
Bum-Bumpity-Bum.

I play it every night
When the fireflies are bright
Boom boom boom boom
Bum-Bumpity-Bum.

But I'm really very proud
That I never play it loud
Boom boom boom boom
Bum-Bumpity-Bum.

Tho' I hardly make a peep,
People say that they can't sleep
Boom boom boom boom
Bum-Bumpity-Bum.

TIM TREACLEKNOTS
——— Acorn Playing Goblin ———

I tried to play a Pussy Cat,
But Pussys won't keep still,
So I fiddle on this acorn
That I found on Primrose Hill.

Does anyone have a Pussy Cat
That will not jump around
When I stretch and play his tail
To make a funkey sound?

If there *is* such a Pussy Cat
A pop star will be born.
Until that day
I'll saw away
On my Primrose Hill Acorn.

TOODLEY GRONICKPET
Goblin Bagpiper

Puff Puff Puff Puff
Into the bag I blow,
Puff Puff Puff Puff,
Ying Tong Iddle I Po.
Puff Puff Puff Puff
I try to fill it with air.
If I don't pump it up
With a hip! and a hup!
I can't get a tune out of there!
So, Puff Puff Puff Puff
Oh what's the use of trying
Whatever tune I try to play
It sound as if I'm dying.

MOCKPELT THRINGDIP
—A Goblin Concertina Player—

No it's not an ocharine
It's a Goblin Concertina,
But play it on your side, oh Chum-chum-chum
For the bellows (made of leather)
Whenever squeezed together
Will double-pleat your poor old Tum-tum-tum.

JACK MIGGER
—A Rock Goblin Raver—

'I'm a rock-and-roll Goblin,
With dancin' feet
A Skooby-do Daddy
From Basin Street,
Ah lurv ma baby,
Ma baby lurvs me,
A bim bam boogie,
And I'm ninety-three'.

So he went a-dancin',
But alas and alack,
He dropped out of the charts,
With a heart attack.

THUG O'BRISTLE
—A Goblin Bouncer—

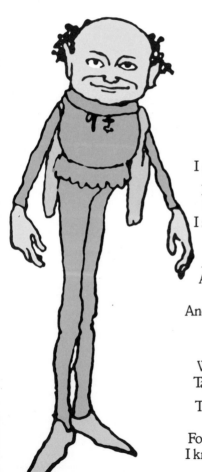

I am a Goblin Bouncer,
I work in a Goblin Pub.
If anyone starts any trouble
I go bash with a dandelion club.

If any one starts to get funny
With the girl behind the bar,
I soon put an end to his nonsense
With a little tinsel star.

And when it comes to closing
And someone refuses to leave,
I grab the man by the collar
And make a red mark on his sleeve.

And if I get very angry
Everyone cringes in fear
While I walk along the counter,
Taking sips from my ginger beer.

That's why we never get trouble
Here in the Piglet and Boar,
For at the first signs of a punch-up
I knock the man down with a straw.

Obolin Foxtip
—A Goblin Juggler—

I'm a Goblin Tommy Cooper,
I can do tricks with a hat,
I can walk upside down with a barrow
So they've made me a Water Rat.

I can juggle with seventy skittles
Dive through a rubber tyre
I can sleep on the bottom of the Channel,
Did somebody call me a liar?

I'm a Goblin Tommy Cooper,
I fly round the room on a mat,
You ask me how do I do it,
I'll tell you, 'Just like that'.

GOLLYNUT BULLSEYE
—A Nutty Goblin—

What in God's name are you trying to do,
Little Sloppy Sam?
'I'm trying to stand on my head for you,
Please will you pass me the jam'.

Why do you want to stand on your head?
It's nearly time for tea.
'I know that quite well, please go to Hell
And pass the celery.'

Look! I must warn you, Sloppy Sam
Your face is going red.
'Of that I'm aware, so please don't stare.
Pray kindly pass the bread!'

Can't you see it's getting quite dark?
The lights are on in town.
'You're perfectly right, please turn out the light
And hand me the eiderdown'.

FRED FERNACKERPAN
—A Mystery Goblin—

I am a mystery fellow,
I'm Fred Fernackerpan,
I wear one sock that's yellow
The other dipped in jam.
I walk about the countryside
I walk about the town,
Sometimes with my trousers up
And sometimes with them down:
And when they were up they were up
And when they were down they were down
And when they were only half way up
He was arrested.

TIM O'PRAFER
—A Catholic Goblin—

'Oh earnest clerical Goblin
How do you get so holy?'
'By saying my prayers in bed at night
And eating roly-poly.'

'Oh earnest clerical Goblin
How long have you been a vicar?'
'No, I'm a Catholic priest', he said,
'Promotion there's much quicker.'

VITUS McSAINT
—A Holy Goblin—

Let's pray for all the sinners
To save them from all Hell,
People burning down below
Don't half bloody yell.

Some will come to a sticky end
For it's been told to me
That some of them fell into the vat
Of the treacle factory.

MILES ANDMOOR
—A Goblin Porter—

Groan groan sweat and strain
Groan and sweat and groan again
Strain and strain and strain some more –
My bottom's nearly on the floor.
Grip, gasp, sweat and groan
Lift and bend and stoop and moan,
Lift and bend and stoop and moan,
'Bejasus – bedad you're doin foin!'
But I've got a lump coming in my groin.

OLIVER SWINEDRENCH
—A Goblin Nutcase—

This is a silly old Charlie,
Wears a black cap and a stick,
He walks about the town all night
And parts of Hampton Wick.
I asked this silly Charlie
What he had in mind,
He said, 'I carry a black stick
So people won't think I'm blind'.
That doesn't explain the skull cap,
'Oh, I've a reason for that.
I wear it because, my dear fellow,
I can't afford a hat'.

CARLO TRATTO-MUNCH
—A Goblin Chef—

I run a Goblin Restaurant,
I make spaghetti and jam,
And although I love it
The diners say, Shove it
Right up your Alikazam!'

I run a Goblin Restaurant
I cook all the food in gin
That's why each diner
Has never felt finer
On the floor looking up with a grin.

LARVEY ACTDROLL
—A Mixed Goblin—

'Are you the old woman who lived in a shoe
Who had so many children you didn't know what to do?
'No, I'm not the old woman who lived in a shoe
Who had so many children she didn't know what to do.
I'm an old man in drag, like Danny la Rue'.

TWERGLER NOTLYSOCKS
—An Aged Goblin—

I'm the eldest Goblin
In the world!
I'm nearly two hundred and seven.
I'm too old to die,
And that is why
I can't go to Hell or to Heaven.

ARG DAFFOSTALK
—A Twit Goblin—

I've got a hole in the top of my head
(On which I have to pay VAT),
The reason it's there
(Surrounded by hair)
Is to help inflate my hat.

By pressing my belly
And shouting out, 'Nelly,'
I force the wind up my skull.
The immediate effect
Is the hat goes erect,
My God, don't you find this all dull.

Tyra Myra Lavaswell
—A Welsh Maiden Goblin—

My first name is Tyra
My second is Myra
And I come from Abergavenny;
By the look in my eye
You would never think I
Had recently poisoned my Granny.

JULIA BRECHTKIN
—A Beautiful Lady Goblin—

I'm such a pretty maiden
But only three inches tall,
So my chances of marriage
Are just not on at all.
Supposing I married a husband
Who was something like five foot three,
On my honeymoon night
I'd die of fright
In case he rolled on me.
But even if I survived it
And set up home in a flat
I don't want to end up each morning
Being brought in by the cat.
So who will marry me? who, oh who?
Only a man of inches two!

ORB VITALITIS
—A Strange Goblin—

In my ruff and habit
And a look as stern as can be
You ask me my ambition
This I say unto ye:

I want to be a Lunatic
A life that's good and free
Your clothes are free, three meals a day,
That's the life for me!

If I stand on a roof with no legs on
Or hang by my teeth from a tree,
If I wear a green hat with pegs on
They'll take no notice of me.

So I want to be a Lunatic
Where life is free from care
It's that or a Member of Parliament –
What sane person wants to be that?

N.B: For best results, reader is asked to stand on
one leg and sing chorus again.

MISS DILLDUMP-POTTS
A Soppy Goblin

Guess which hand I've got it in,
Is it left or right?
I've got to leave here by nine o'clock
So please don't take all night.
So hurry please hurry and tell me!
Wait! I know what to do!
The hand that's empty I'll open,
That ought to give you a clue.

LADY CHICKEN-PECK
——A Mature Lady Goblin——

I'm staring into the future
And the future is staring back
And it says to me,
'You're forty-three
Oh woe! Alas! Alack!'
So I'm staring into the past
Looking over my shoulder
And it says to me,
'Yes, you're forty-three
And you're going to get much older!'

LUMPKIN GRONIC
——————An Ill Goblin——————

Lumpkin Gronic
Wanted a tonic
To try and make him happy.
'These valium pills
Will cure your ills',
Said Dr Grippy-Grappy.

So he swallowed the lot,
The lid and pot
But didn't get much better.
Then, after dark
He started to bark,
By dawn he'd become A Red Setter.

—OTIS SNIFT—
A Goblin Funeral Director

I'm a Goblin Mortician,
That's why I'm wearing black,
I drive 'em off to the grave-yard
But I never bring 'em back.

People are quite tearful
When relatives end their day
But honestly, it cheers me up
To see 'em drive away.

And now I give the reason
I say it with misgiving:
To some people what they call death
I will call a living.

GROPKIN LOL
—A Goblin Banker—

I'm adding my bank statement
And it is a terrible bore!
I've been adding up since the early dawn
To see if I'm rich or poor.

So one and one are two
Two and two are four,
No matter how many times I try
I can't make it any more!

ETHEO E COWAN
—A Jewish Goblin—

I am a Kosher Goblin
'Good luck', I hear you say?
I run a little schmutter shop
In Golders Green, 'Oi Vey!'

I got another schmutter shop,
'Och Aye' to them I say.
Why oh why, do I say, 'Och Aye?'
It's Golders Greenock way.

EVASMUS G. CLOCK
—A Mystery Goblin—

I am something or other
Which one, I am not sure!
I'm either a sister or brother,
I'm either rich or poor,
I'm either a Scot or a Zulu,
I'm either like sherry or port,
But I'm *not* a fox or a pheasant,
So *please* don't shoot me for sport.

'BLUEY' TIGWORT
——A Dinkum Goblin——

I am a Goblin Swaggie,
I'm going to Australia
I leave old England shores tonight
For here I've been a failure.

So farewell Goblin Swaggie,
Set fair for Melbourne City
If you're a failure there as well
Don't ask the Poms for pity.

THE TRIANGLE GOBLIN

Ting a ling a ling
Can you help me, friend?
I've lost touch with my Goblin Band
Marching to Land's End.

Ting a ling a ling
I lost them near Goonhilly,
But they're bound to stop when they reach Land's End,
To go further would be Scilly!

STIRLING DISTRICT LIBRARY

Book design by Bernard Higton

Hutchinson & Co (Publishers) Ltd
3 Fitzroy Square, London W1P 6JD

London Melbourne Sydney Auckland Wellington Johannesburg
and agencies throughout the world

Text first published 1978
© Spike Milligan Productions Ltd

Illustrations first published in
Heath Robinson's Book of Goblins 1934
© Oliver Robinson
Printed and bound in Great Britain by
William Clowes and Sons Ltd, Newgate, Beccles, Suffolk.

ISBN 0 09 131920 X